MBA ASAP
10 minutes to:

Understanding Corporate Finance

John Cousins

FREE DOWNLOAD

MBA ASAP 10 Minutes to

Understanding Financial Statements

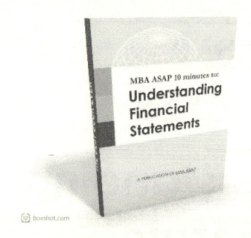

Go to www.mba-asap.com

and click on the big orange button

TABLE OF CONTENTS

MBA ASAP

INTRODUCTION

Finance is a broad topic that can be challenging to wrap your mind around. For clarity's sake, think of Finance of organized along economic lines of micro and macro. On the micro side we have business decisions and Corporate Finance. On the macro side we have financial markets, money and banking.

This book will focus on Corporate Finance. Corporate Finance covers how to analyze opportunities. It provides tools to make decisions like what projects to pursue and how to value those projects. This book provides a framework for how to make decisions about how, when, and where to invest money.

Corporate finance is concerned with making allocation decisions about limited resources. A business has human resources, technical resources, and access to money. It wants to put those resources to work to take advantage of opportunities to grow and make money. The task of management is to allocate and leverage the resources it controls.

Management must choose the most promising projects. That is how their performance gets measured. That is how they are rewarded. That is how they keep their jobs.

Managers and leaders want to make supportable rational decisions about what to do and how to do it. They also need to track the performance of their decisions. And course correct when necessary. Corporate finance provides a set of tools for informing these decisions.

Corporate Finance skills interact with all the aspects of running a business. These tools and techniques are also helpful in our personal lives. We make decisions about buying or leasing, borrowing money, and making big purchases. Armed with this knowledge, make better decisions about spending, saving, and investing money.

In this book we will explore the time value of money. We will learn how to use Net Present Value and Internal Rate of Return.

We will examine the trade off between risk and return, and how to value income producing assets. Valuation of companies and assets can seem mysterious. Where do you even begin? How can you value a startup that doesn't even have any revenues yet? By the end of this book you will be able to answer those questions.

You will gain confidence in your knowledge and understanding of finance. The tools of corporate finance will help you as a manager or business owner. You will make smart decisions about the value of opportunities that come your way. You will know which ones to pursue.

Understanding corporate finance is essential for the professional manager. Numbers are the language of business. Take part in decisions with colleagues and upper management. You need command of this subject to climb any corporate ladder.

Let's begin by looking at financial statement analysis and ratios.

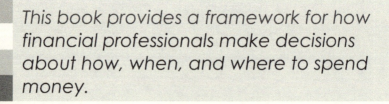

This book provides a framework for how financial professionals make decisions about how, when, and where to spend money.

Chapter One

Ratio Analysis

RATIO ANALYSIS

There are essentially two basic techniques that are used in Corporate Finance. One is the ratio analysis of financial statements and the other is calculating the present value of future cash flows. Bankers, investors, financiers, CFOs and entrepreneurs use these tools and techniques to value assets and make investment decisions.

We can think of these two basic techniques like driving a car. Ratio analysis use the accounting data provided in financial statements. Financial statements are summations of prior activities. So they are like looking in a rear view mirror.

Lets look at using financial ratios as a capital budgeting tool. There are lots of different accounting ratios that get used inside of a firm. In fact, a lot of times the same accounting ratio gets called different things at different firms.

By ratio analysis I mean taking two numbers from financial statements and dividing one by the other. What we are doing is taking two pieces of accounting data, put one over the other, and this forms a ratio. We are taking two pieces of data and forming a performance metric. Ratios are usually presented as a percentage or a number depending on whether the usual case is bigger or less than one.

Ratios allow us to compare different companies or a company over time. Ratios are great tools to do this comparison because they allow us to "normalize" the numbers. A ratio eliminates any size differences and allows for pure comparison so you can compare apples to apples.

For this reason, ratio analysis is the basis for the stock market investment strategy of value investing. Value investing is the discipline of examining and comparing companies based on their relative value and determining whether they are a bargain or expensive.

Financial ratios are derived from accounting information and rely on an understanding of financial statements.

There are three basic financial statements:

Balance Sheet

Income Statement

Cash Flow Statement

They are interconnected and financial data and information flows from one financial statement through the others.

Current financial statements represent a picture of where the company is today. It's a picture of how the company has performed in the most recent reporting period. Financial statements are how the present is connected to the past in business.

If you need a primer or refresher on understanding financial statements check out my *10 Minute Series* book on the subject.

A particularly common valuation of companies done by ratio analysis is based on multiples of Earnings. The Price/Earnings ratio, or P/E for short, is a way companies are compared based on their stock price relative to their earnings. The earnings number is the bottom line of the Income Statement. Earnings are also referred to as Net Income or Profit.

This ratio works well for comparing public companies that report these numbers. This technique can also be used to value a private company by comparing its earnings and valuation range to an average of public reporting companies in similar industry sectors and markets.

Other common ratios based on the Balance Sheet are Return on Equity (ROE) and Return on Assets (ROA). A company can basically be thought of as a bunch of income producing assets. How much income they produce relative to how much they cost to acquire is a measure of how well they are performing.

Assets are bought using two types of funds, Equity, which is money investors put in, and Debt, which is borrowed from a bank or other lender. The Debt-to-Equity Ratio measures how much a company is borrowing.

We can use ROE and ROA to analyze the performance of the Assets of a company. Here we take the money generated by the income producing assets and divide it by Equity for ROE or total assets for ROA.

Ratio analysis is a powerful tool for investing in the stock market. If you like the idea of being a player in stock market and making good investments, check out The Intelligent Investor by Benjamin Graham. It is the bible of value investing and it's the way Warren Buffett and other successful investors do it.

A financial ratio eliminates any size differences and allows for pure comparison so you can compare apples to apples.

Chapter Two

Time Value of Money

TIME VALUE OF MONEY

There are two sets of data that we use in corporate finance: retrospective and prospective. Retrospective data is compiled in financial statements. These represent the historical performance of an enterprise and can be analyzed, compared, and extrapolated. Ratios are the tools of financial statement analysis and we just discussed them. In our driving analogy they are the rear view mirror.

Prospective data is compiled in financial projections. Projections are like looking at the road through the windshield. These represent management's forecast of how the enterprise will perform in the future. These projections can be analyzed, risk adjusted, and a present value of those future cash flows can be calculated. We will now get into the forward-looking aspects of finance with the concept of the time value of money (TVM).

Time is money, literally. If there is a prospect of receiving a certain sum, then the sooner you receive it, the more it is worth. **Interest rates** describe this relationship between present value and future value. This is the fundamental concept of finance. We will explore this relationship between present and future value from different angles and I will phrase it in different ways in order to let it sink in.

TVM represents the conceptual basis of finance. This is the underlying principle of how banks function, how stocks and bonds are priced, how assets and companies are valued, how projects are analyzed, and how you should think about the nature and function of money.

The Time Value of Money is the Fundamental Principle of Finance

A bird in the hand is worth two in the bush. Receiving money today is worth more than getting the same amount in the future; and the value of the prospect of receiving money diminishes the further into the future the promise to deliver money. The rate at which the value of a dollar in the future decreases relative to a dollar today is inversely proportional to the rate at which a dollar invested today will increase in the future. Take a second to let that point sink in. The future and the present value are two sides of the same coin (pun intended!) and they are related to each other by the interest rate.

The concept of the time value of money explains why interest is paid or earned. Interest, whether it is on a bank deposit or debt, compensates the depositor or lender for the time value of money. Risk has to do with uncertainty. There is uncertainty of being repaid as a lender and uncertainty of future profits as a stock investor. Interest rates and required rates of return reflect the level of uncertainty or risk. One of the reasons credit cards carry such high interest rates is that the risk of other people defaulting on their balance is baked into the rate you pay.

The monetary linchpin between the present and the future is interest rates or discount rates. If you have a present value and you want to calculate a future value, we call it an interest rate. If you have future values and you want to estimate their worth today, we use a discount rate. Interest rates and discount rates are two sides of the same coin, to use a money metaphor.

The concept of Time Value of Money also underlies investment in stocks, bonds, or startups. Investing is about managing risk versus return. An investor is willing to forego spending their money now if they expect a favorable return on their investment in the future. The return required is related to the perceived risk of getting one's money back in the future; the higher the perceived risk, the higher the required rate of return. An investor is willing to part with their precious capital when greed overcomes fear; where the expected return exceeds the perceived risk.

MARTINVS NAVARRVS AB ASPILCVETA.
His etiam merito Doctor Martine tabellis
Conspiceris genij ob regia dona tui:
Rex ditis ingenio, rex codice iuris vtroque,
Hispano regi iure Nauarre, places.

8

History Lesson

The concept of the time value of money dates back to the 1500s. Martín de Azpilcueta (December 13, 1491 – June 1, 1586), also known as Doctor Navarrus, was a Basque theologian and an early economist. He was the first person to develop a theory of money. He invented the mathematical concept of the time value of money. It's an idea that's about 500 years old.

Chapter Three

Discounting Cash Flows

DISCOUNTING CASH FLOWS

The core of corporate finance is calculating the present value of future cash flows. This concept is based on the time value of money. A company is essentially an entity that generates cash flows each year into the future. The trick is estimating those future cash flows and how much they might grow or shrink and what the risks are to realizing (i.e. receiving) them.

It's difficult to peer into the fog of the future. This is where you have to polish your crystal ball and do some deep analysis of the business, its markets and competitors. All this information is compiled in a spreadsheet of financial projections and the bottom line represents the future cash flows in each year. These are discounted back to the present value at a discount rate that takes into account what similar investments, which are just streams of expected cash flows, are priced at in the market and any and all risks specific to the particular enterprise or asset we are contemplating buying or selling.

This is the basic concept of Valuation. Valuation is an estimate of something's worth. Something's worth can be set at auction where people bid and the highest bidder wins. But how do bidders know how much to bid and how much is too much? For income producing assets, like stocks, it's the present value of the future cash flows.

The stock market is essentially an auction where investors place **Bids**: how much they are willing to pay for a stock, and **Asks**: how much an investor is willing to sell for. When a Bid and Ask match, a transaction happens and a new price is set. Companies and assets, and even startups that don't have any revenues yet, are valued using this principle.

This technique of calculating the present value of a stream of cash flows becomes essential when trying to value start-ups that have no revenue history or assets, or companies that are predicted to grow rapidly. In these cases you can't rely on past performance and history in order to come up with a value based on P/E or their existing assets.

Discounting Cash Flows (DCF) is the technique favored by investment bankers, venture capitalists, private equity, hedge funds, savvy investors, banks and credit analysts, and CFOs. It's not difficult to understand and you will be amazed how useful and powerful it can be.

Let's go through an example.

DISCOUNTING CASH FLOWS
Present Value and Future Value

$100 invested for one year, earning 5% interest, will be worth $105 after one year; therefore, $100 paid now and $105 paid exactly one year later both have the same value to a recipient who expects 5% return. That is, $100 invested for one year at 5% interest has a future value of $105. This assumes that inflation is zero percent and doesn't contribute to eroding the value.

The equation in this case would look like this:

$105 = $100 * (1+.05)

The general formula for solving for future value is:

$$FV = PV * (1+r)$$

Where FV is future value, PV is present value, and r is the interest rate

The reciprocal formula, to solve for present value, juggles the terms using basic algebra and restates the relationship as:

$$PV = FV/(1+r)$$

It simply puts the (1+r) term on the other side of the equation to solve for PV by dividing both sides by (1+r). If this is confusing just replace (1+r) by the term X for the moment.

FV = PV * X

If you divide both sides by X you get: FV/X = PV * X/X

Since the term X/X is equal to one, the term goes away on that side of the equation. So we are left with: FV/X = PV

Now replace the X with (1+r) and you see the derivation of our equation.

Take a moment to make sure you really understand this because it is the basis of project finance and asset valuation. This is the formula we use to calculate future cash flows as a present value.

This concept is used to calculate the value today of a projected stream of income in the future.

Sit with this page for a while until these concepts are clear. **This is the core concept of finance.**

$$PV = FV / (1+i)^n$$

PV = present value

FV = future value (money to be received in the future)

i = discount rate

n = number of periods until FV is received

Above is the general formula for calculating Present Value. All the terms are familiar from the previous page except the exponent n, which represents the year in which the particular payment is due.

For example if the Future Value was due in year 2 then n would be 2; if the Future Value was due in year 5 then n would be 5.

The further out in time, the bigger n is and the more discounting is applied to FV.

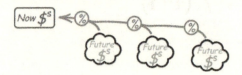

When there is a stream of FVs, these cash flows are all discounted based on the year they are coming in and then added together. The sum is the present value of the entire income stream.

Chapter Four

Net Present Value

NET PRESENT VALUE

Now that we have gone over the conceptual basis of Corporate Finance we are going to look at the main techniques and tools used in financial analysis and decision-making.

In business we invest in projects that make money in the future. We pay now and intend to reap the rewards in the future. Usually a project or asset will make money as a stream of revenues and profits over years. It could also be a project whose main benefit is savings. We need the ability to calculate whether that stream of future cash flows is worth more than the money we need to invest to buy it or build it.

The way we look at decisions about whether to fund a project or calculate the value of an asset is to turn that stream of future dollars into today's dollars. Then we compare that sum of present values to the cost; if the cost is more than the total present value, we don't do the deal; if it is less, it is considered a good investment.

This is the way projects are analyzed and assessed as go or no go, and how income producing assets and acquisitions are valued for sale or purchase.

So far we have analyzed and calculated the value of future cash flows and brought them back to present value. **Net Present Value** (NPV) takes this idea a step further and accounts for the transactional aspect. We must "purchase" the future cash flows either by:

- Buying a bond or stock, or
- Acquiring a company, or
- Purchasing an income-producing asset, or
- Undertaking a project and incurring the costs of developing or building the income-producing asset.

Net present value "nets out" the cost of acquiring the future cash flows. NPV compares the cost in today's dollars to the present value of projected future income or benefits also in today's dollars. Its only worth doing if the price is less than our present value assessment of the future benefits.

NPV is the main tool used to value assets and make decisions about projects, purchases, mergers, or acquisitions. The spreadsheets can get pretty complicated when they are populated with all the costs, revenue and expense projections, and assumptions about timing and risk, but the basic idea is always to compare the costs to the future benefits and compare them apples to apples by taking into account the time value of money.

NPV answers a simple question: does the present value of all the money coming in over the life of the project outweigh how much money we have to spend in order to receive it? Net present value is just that, it's the net between the present value of these two streams: the money going out and the money coming in.

We ask whether NPV is greater than 0. If it's greater than 0, then the costs are less than the benefits and we should do the project or make the investment.

That's our decision rule: is the NPV bigger than 0? We can construct the formula for NPV by following along very closely with what we did in our discussion of discounting cash flows.

The NPV is equal to the initial cost, which has a minus sign in front of it, plus the present value of what's coming in off the project as cash flows. Cash flow in period 1, discounted one period back, plus the cash flow in period two, discounted two periods back, the cash flow in period 3, discounted back three periods, you get the idea, plus all the other cash flows coming in discounted by their period.

What we do is take that initial cost and weigh that against the present value of all the cash coming in. We're going to "net" the two. There's a minus sign on the costs, and plus signs on all of the present value cash flows.

We ask how all the money going out weighs against all the money coming in. Think of it like a balance. If we know the initial investment and the stream of money coming in from the project in the future, we can measure the NPV as the difference between the two; the net between those two streams.

As the initial investment becomes larger, the NPV become smaller. You can see that the NPV, whether it's bigger than 0 or less than 0, depends on that balance between the money going out and the money coming in. Let's work a problem and compute an NPV in practice.

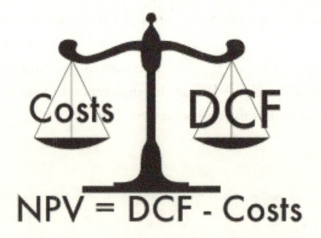

NPV = DCF - Costs

Analyze the table of cash flows below and compute the NPV if the discount rate is 15%

EXAMPLE PROJECT

	Today			
Year:	0	1	2	Sum (NPV)
	-$3,000	$1,500	$1800	$300

Let's think about whether it's worth it to do this project. In period 0, today; we need to spend $3,000. Is it worth it to spend that $3,000? What do we expect to get in return?

What are the cash flows coming in off the project? We have a cash flow of $1,500 coming in at the end of year one. And we've got a cash flow of $1,800 coming in at the end of year two. If we just sum up the cash flows, a minus 3000 (it is minus because it is a cost) plus 1500 plus 1800, we get an answer of $300. This project is generating cash. It's profitable. The money coming in is bigger than the money going out.

That's the sum of all the cash flows, but that's without any discounting. We haven't accounted for the fact that we have to wait a year to get the $1,500. And then wait another year after that to get the $1,800. Remember: to use money you have to pay; there is a cost of capital. So what do we have to pay? In this case, we have to pay that 15% discount rate. That is the cost of capital in this example. 15% is our hurdle rate.

Today

Year:	0	1	2	Sum (NPV)
	-$3,000	$1,500	$1800	$300

Present

Value: $\quad 1500/(1.15)^1 \quad 1800/(1.15)^2$

NPV

@15% -$3,000 + $1,304.35 + $1,361.06 = **-$334.59**

We need to adjust the cash flows for the time value of money by discounting them to the present value. We take that $1,500 and discount it one period at 15% and we get $1,304.35. Then we take the $1,800 and discount it two periods at 15% and we get $1,361.06. Now when we sum the present value of all those cash flows, we get **minus** $334.59, which tells us that the project destroys value. It's not worth doing.

It's a profitable project, but we don't want to do it. We will pass. Why would we ever *not* want to do a project that's profitable? It all comes down to the 15% discount rate. That 15% indicates what the hurdle rate is for the profitability of the project. This project might be profitable, but it is not profitable enough to justify the required 15% return. If our investors require a 15% return to take the risk of that project, we're not going to be able to deliver it to them with a project like this.

Let's examine the main drivers in that net present value calculation. First is cash flow. More cash is better than less. The second is the timing. The further the cash flow is out in the future, the deeper it gets discounted.

And the third driver is the discount rate. The higher the discount rate, the deeper the cash flows get discounted and the lower the NPV. The lower the discount rate, the less discounting, the better the project. Lower discount rates, higher NPV. Higher discount rates, lower NPV.

Net present value is the benchmark metric. It is our best capital budgeting tool. It incorporates the timing of the cash flows. It incorporates the opportunity cost. The opportunity cost is the cost we incur by committing to this project and forgoing other options that could make us money. That discount rate quantifies, in essence, what else could we do with the money.

The fact that we're discounting implicitly incorporates the opportunity cost. And it incorporates risk. If we think the project is a lot riskier, what can we do to incorporate that in our analysis? We can increase the discount rate to reflect that risk.

NPV is objective. It is not concerned with whether we "like" the project or not. It relies on the quality of our forecasting discount rates. We can lay this out and calculate it in a way that is presentable and explainable to anybody. It's an arm's length metric. NPV is transparent. We could sit down together with a spreadsheet and go over it and explain all the assumptions to each other. This process allows us to test the veracity of our assumptions and get buy-in from others.

Net present value weighs the costs and benefits of cash coming in versus cash going out. NPV gives us an objective, arm's length, and transparent metric for capital budgeting.

$$NPV = -C_0 + C_1/(1+i) + C_2/(1+i)^2 + \ldots + C_T/(1+i)^T$$

$-C0$ = Initial Investment

C = Cash Flow

i = Discount rate

T = Time

The main drivers of NPV are:

- **Cash Flow**. Obviously, more cash is better than less.
- **Timing**. The further the cash flow is out in the future, the deeper it gets discounted.
- **Discount Rate**. The higher the discount rate, the deeper the cash flows get discounted and the lower the NPV. The lower the discount rate, the less discounting, the better the project. Lower discount rates, higher NPV. Higher discount rates, lower NPV.

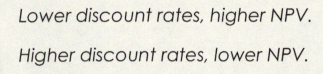

Lower discount rates, higher NPV.

Higher discount rates, lower NPV.

Net present value weighs the costs and benefits of cash coming in versus cash going out, and gives us an objective, arm's length, and transparent metric for capital budgeting.

Chapter Five

Internal
Rate of Return

INTERNAL RATE OF RETURN

Next we are going to explore using the Internal Rate of Return (IRR) as a capital budgeting tool. We will explore how to use it for deciding how to best to invest money and allocate resources.

Internal rate of return is derivative of NPV. **Internal rate of return is the discount rate that makes the NPV from a particular project equal to zero.** The higher the internal rate of return of a proposed project, the more desirable the project.

NPV tells us whether the present value of the cash coming in exceeds the cash going out. NPV calculates the net of the present value of the cash flows. With IRR we come at the issue from a different angle.

First we compute an NPV and then we ask what discount rate sets the NPV equal to 0. The discount rate that makes the cash outflow equal to the present value of the cash inflows is the IRR. Our decision rule with IRR is we're going to invest if that rate is bigger than our hurdle rate.

Internal rate of return is solving for how much we need to discount the cash flows in order to drive the value out of the project. It's a measure of the resiliency of the cash flows. It measures the capacity of the project to withstand and recover from difficulties.

The more we discount, the more that drives down the NPV. How much do we have to discount it and still stay bigger than 0? That's what IRR tells us. This decision rule is similar to our net present value decision, as we'll see graphically.

IRR takes the Net Present Value, which is a numerical value, and restates it as a percentage. This makes it more intuitive and comprehensible.

It's difficult for us to grasp the meaning of a large number. It has little context. If I say the NPV is $3,537,000 it means little by itself. If I tell you the internal rate of return on the project is 25%, it's easy to intuitively grasp. It takes the net present value and converts it into a percentage that's easier to grasp and understand.

It gives us a more intuitive and appealing take on the NPV of a project. IRR doesn't tell the whole story though and it's best to always use it in conjunction with NPV. We will discuss caveats related to IRR later. NPV provides the scale and IRR provides the intuition.

Let's examine IRR in formulaic terms. When we discussed the net present value formula, NPV was equal to the initial cost weighed against all of the cash flows in future years.

$$NPV = - \text{Initial Costs} + CF_1/(1+r) + CF_2/(1+r)^2 + CF_3/(1+r)^3 \ldots.$$

That is our formula for NPV. To calculate IRR we're going to take that formula and replace r the discount rate, with IRR and set that equal to 0. The discount rate that sets this series of numbers equal to 0 is the IRR.

$$0 = - \text{Initial Costs} + CF_1/(1+IRR) + CF_2/(1+IRR)^2 + CF_3/(1+IRR)^3 \ldots.$$

Remember there is a minus sign in front of the Initial Costs.

It's difficult and time consuming to solve the polynomial equation for IRR with pen and paper. There is no direct calculation. It is an iterative process. You make a guess, do the calculation, and adjust as you overshoot or undershoot the mark. Here is the formula to get an idea of how cumbersome it is to populate and calculate.

Internal Rate of Return

n = number of cash flows

CF_i = cash flow at period j.

IRR = Internal Rate of Return

$$0 = \sum_{j=1}^{k} CF_j \cdot \left[\frac{1-(1+IRR)^{-n_j}}{IRR} \right] \cdot \left[(1+IRR)^{-\sum\limits_{q<j} n_q} \right] + CF_0$$

As you can well imagine, IRR was not a very useful tool before financial calculators, computers and spreadsheets.

But it's easy to do in a spreadsheet or on a financial calculator. They have IRR functions built in. Here is an example from Excel. You just put in the range of cash flows and make a guess at the IRR. The computer will chug through the calculations and provide the answer in a split second.

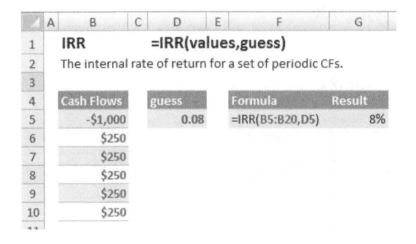

	A	B	C	D	E	F	G
1		IRR		=IRR(values,guess)			
2		The internal rate of return for a set of periodic CFs.					
3							
4		Cash Flows		guess		Formula	Result
5		-$1,000		0.08		=IRR(B5:B20,D5)	8%
6		$250					
7		$250					
8		$250					
9		$250					
10		$250					

I prefer Excel or a spreadsheet program on a computer because you can build out the model and save the results. This is important if later your boss or client asks how you came up with that number. Always save your work for later reference.

Let's look at the relationship between NPV and IRR graphically. Here we have a project that has a positive NPV and we graph the value of the net present value in dollars.

As we discount the cash flows with progressively higher and higher discount rates, the NPV declines. At some point, it crosses 0. The point at which NPV crosses 0, the discount rate that sets NPV equal to 0, is the IRR.

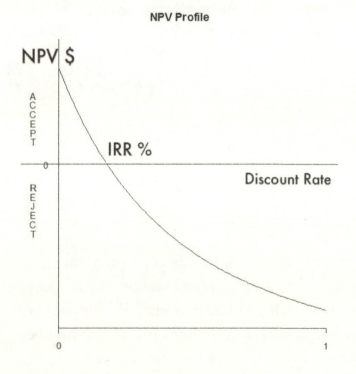

NPV Profile

Any time the discount rate is below the IRR, it's a positive NPV project. So if our hurdle rate is 7% and the IRR is 12% it's judged a good project. IRR is similar to NPV, except that we have discounted the cash flows to a percentage rate where the discounting just crosses to negative, at 0.

IRR = Internal Rate of Return
IRR = Rate at Which NPV = $0

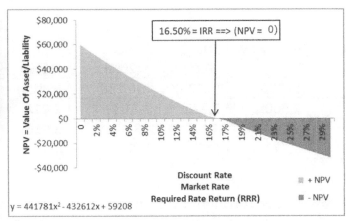

16.50% = IRR ==> (NPV = 0)

$y = 441781x^2 - 432612x + 59208$

Now we can say, for example, the return on this project, the IRR, is 12%. That is easier to understand than saying the net present value is $1,613,672, which is just a big number with no context. We don't have a good idea what it means. But if the return is 12%, we can compare: 12% relative to a 7% cost on capital. We have a comparison. That's a good project.

IRR Example

Time	Cash Flow	Trial 1 (10%)	Trial 2 (20%)	Trial 3 (13%)
0	(6,128)	(6,128)	(6,128)	(6,128)
1	2,500	2,273	2,083	2,212
2	5,000	4,132	3,472	3,916
NPV	1,372	277	-572	**0**

Let's think this through with an example. Let's say we were spending $6,128 to generate cash of $2,500 in year one, and $5,000 in year two. If we don't do any discounting at all and just add up the cash flows that would be $1,372.

Now lets discount the cash flows at 10%. We discount the $2,500 back one period at 10%, and discount the $5,000 back two periods at 10%. That gives us a net present value of $277.

If instead of discounting at 10%, we discounted at 20%, we get a net present value of **minus** $572. So what must have happened somewhere in between?

At some point the net present value crossed from positive to negative. If we solve it, that actually happens at 13%. That's the point where we are discounting it enough to draw all the value out of it.

In the above example we keep guessing and solving for different discount rates until we converge on an answer. IRR is a really easy thing to calculate in Excel. Built into Excel is an IRR function. There are many tutorials online that will show you how to use that function. It solves the polynomial equation, finds the root, sets it to 0, and gives us the solution automatically.

IRR confounds easy math solutions. There is no formula for IRR where you can plug in the numbers and calculate the solution. You calculate IRR via an iterative process of trial and error. Each successive iteration gets closer and finally converges on the solution. This type of convergence algorithm is what computers excel at.

Microsoft Excel does it by crunching through thousands of calculations. Before spreadsheets you could estimate IRR with cross-reference tables. Now with a few mouse clicks, we get an accurate IRR solution.

IRR is a really easy thing to calculate in Excel. Built into Excel is an IRR function. There are many tutorials online that will show you how to use that function. It solves the polynomial equation, finds the root, sets it to 0, and gives us the solution automatically.

IRR accounts for the timing, the opportunity cost, and the risk of a project in a similar way to NPV. IRR is a good capital budgeting tool but it should not be relied upon as a standalone measure. We should always compute it alongside of the gold standard NPV.

IRR Shortfalls and Caveats

IRR provides insight. It's an intuitive way to grasp the value of a stream of cash flows, but there are a couple of caveats. IRR is a summary type of number. As with all summaries, compressing the solution squeezes out information. By reducing the solution to a percentage IRR is easy to grasp. But there are issues surrounding the information that gets eliminated.

NPV is our gold standard capital budgeting tool. IRR is like NPV. We have looked at the similarities and differences, as well as the benefits of including IRR in our analysis.

IRR has a couple of complications in practice that we will now look at.

The first case is when cash flows in a stream get reversed. When they come in and go out, come in and go out, IRR can get confused for some math reasons that we will look at.

When Cash Flows are Reversed During a Project

IRR can be misleading when cash flows reverse from positive to negative during a project. In a situation where money comes in and then money goes out, the sign, negative and positive, flips. Any time cash flows flip negative and positive in a stream of cash flows, we need to be careful using IRR.

Lets use a machine acquisition as an example. We acquire a machine and the machine generates revenue. Then we have to retool the machine in year three and we spend more cash. Then it generates more revenue. That's two sign changes. There is money out for the initial purchase, money in, money out for the retooling, and then more money in. Any time the cash flow direction flips a couple of times; IRR can give us confusing results.

Borrower Type Loan Flow IRR Example

Project	CF$_0$	CF$_1$	IRR	NPV @ 10%
A	(400)	500	25%	54.54
B	400	(500)	25%	(54.54)

Consider these two projects, A and B. In the first, we are going to spend $400 to generate $500 a year from now. In this case the NPV comes out to $54.54 and the IRR comes out to 25%. In the second project we've got $400 coming in, and then spend $500 a year from now. This stream looks like a loan from the borrower's side. We are getting money in, and paying it back later. In the case of project B, the net present value is **negative** $54.54. It is the inverse scenario of Project A. In this case, we aren't making $54; we are losing $54. But when we calculate IRR, it's the same 25%.

Did something get messed up? No, the math is correct. Remember IRR is the interest rate that sets NPV to zero. This is the point where the costs are equal to the present value of the future cash flows. The solution to what rate sets NPV equal to 0 is 25%. But the NPV has flipped from positive to negative. We need be careful any time there's a flip in the sign of the cash flows.

Let's look at it from the graph perspective. For project A the NPV is downward sloping and above zero until it crosses at the IRR. But in project B the NPV is negative and upward sloping until it crosses zero at the IRR.

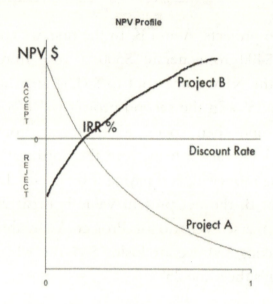

NPV Profile

They have the same IRR. But for a low discount rate, project B is going to give us a negative NPV, whereas project A is going to give us a positive NPV. At a high discount rate, Project B is NPV positive. IRR really gets confused when there are multiple changes in cash flow direction in a stream.

The solution is to always put IRR next to NPV. If you compute an IRR, compare it with the net present value. NPV always serves as a check on whether you're getting the right capital budgeting decision.

Scale and IRR

Another issue is comparing the scale of different projects or investments using IRR. If we have mutually exclusive projects that we want to compare and decide between, it's hard to meaningfully compare them with IRR alone. Mutually exclusive means we can't pursue all proposed projects because of limited resources. We must choose one or the other. In choosing one, we must forgo the other. A financial officer's job is to decide to pursue the best opportunities that generate the most money.

It's not clear whether a higher IRR indicates a higher NPV. Let's go through an example of how we would compare mutually exclusive projects with the IRR.

Project	CF$_0$	CF$_1$	IRR	NPV @ 10%
1	(1)	2	100%	0.82
2	(100)	120	20%	9.1

In project 1 we are just going to spend $1. This would represent a modest incremental project. That's going to generate $2 in period 1.

That looks like a great project from an IRR standpoint. We are spending $1 in order to make $2. That's a 100% IRR!

Or we could also choose project 2. That would cost $100, and would generate $120. That is only a 20% IRR.

It looks like project 1 is better than project 2 in terms of adding value, because it's got such a bigger IRR.

But if we compute the net present value, project 1 generates $0.82. Project 2 generates $9.10. Project 2 has a much bigger NPV. We should do Project 2.

Project 2 is much better from a net present value standpoint. It's generating a lot more value in total dollars for the firm. It's just that project 1 is generating a relatively higher IRR number. IRR doesn't take the scale of the project into account.

The best way to avoid being misled is, again, to put IRR next to NPV. That checks whether IRR is meets our hurdle rate *and* whether the scale is giving us the right decision.

We can analyze this graphically by looking at two projects. Projects A and B have the same IRR, but Project A has a much higher net present value. Project A is preferable to Project B. For all discount rates less than the IRR, it's going to generate more NPV.

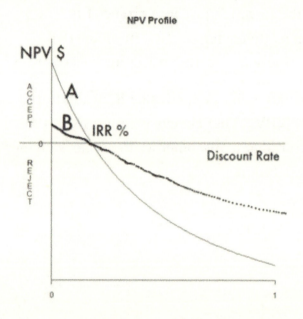

Always put that IRR next to a net present value in order to check for scale issues.

Multiple or No Solution to IRR

Situations exist where there is no solution to the IRR polynomial.

If you put the cash flows into the IRR formula in Excel and it won't give you an answer, it could be that there's multiple IRRs or no solution.

Project	CF$_0$	CF$_1$	CF$_2$	IRR
A	(100)	235	136	[5%, 30%]
B	(100)	120	(50)	- -

Consider the example above. We are analyzing two projects. In both projects we spend 100. In Project A we plan to make 235 in year 1 and 136 in year 2. Project B is forecast to make 120 and negative 50.

In Project A there are actually two IRR's, not one. In Project B there is no IRR.

IRR is the solution to a math equation and there are scenarios where there is no solution to the math problem. Graphically, Project A and B look like this: for Project A the NPV gets bigger for a while, then starts to go down. This project has two IRR's. NPV crosses zero twice as the discount rate increases.

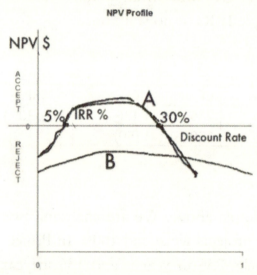

It could also be the case that a project is such a total loser that it never gets up to a positive NPV. That is the case with Project B. It has no IRR because it never crosses zero.

Once again, how do we address this issue? Make sure to compare an IRR calculation to a net present value. This way you can always check whether IRR is giving you the right capital budgeting decision.

Shortfalls of IRR Summary

IRR is a good capital budgeting tool. But it is not a standalone measure. IRR alone can be misleading because of:

- The nature of mutually exclusive projects,
- The scale problem,
- Cash flow timing issues,
- Whether or not there's an answer or solution

Always check IRR next to the net present value. As long as you aware of these caveats and compare IRR to the NPV, IRR is a legitimate analysis tool. IRR provides intuitive insight. It helps us get an idea of what the return on the project is relative to the discount rate.

CONCLUSION

Corporations and investors invest in real assets that are intended to be productive in generating income. Some of these assets such as apartment buildings, factories, offices, machinery and computers are tangible. Others such as brand names and patents are intangible.

The decision-making tools of corporate finance assess the value of proposed projects and income producing assets based on the time value of money and its relation to risk. We rank projects based on the present value of their future cash flows. How we do that is called discounted cash flow (DCF) valuation.

Lets take stock of the capital budgeting tools that we've talked about:

- Net present value
- IRR
- Accounting ratios

CFOs rely on multiple metrics when making capital budgeting decisions. There are pros and cons to IRR, net present value and accounting ratios. What is important to understand is that each one of those data points represents an interesting and informative perspective.

Using a portfolio of different capital budgeting tools helps make for better financial decisions. NPV is the gold standard.

We can also use earnings multiples and other accounting ratios that we talked about. They can provide interesting information but should not be solely relied upon in making capital budgeting decisions. Always include NPV and IRR. Include IRR and NPV next to ROE or ROA so that you can make a more informed and better decision.

Use these capital budgeting tools that have a solid theoretical and empirical foundation and start making better financial decisions.

MBA ASAP

FREE DOWNLOAD

MBA ASAP 10 Minutes to

Understanding Financial Statements

Go to www.mba-asap.com and click on the big orange button

Thank you for reading!

Dear Reader,

I hope you enjoyed **MBA ASAP 10 Minutes to: Understanding Corporate Finance** and found it filled with useful and valuable information..

As an author, I love feedback. Candidly, you are the reason that I organize my thoughts, write, and explore these topics. So, tell me what you liked, what was helpful and what could be better explained or left out. You can write me at john.counsins@mba-asap.com and visit me on the web at www.mba-asap.com.

Finally, I need to ask a favor. If you're so inclined, I'd love a review on Amazon of **MBA ASAP 10 Minutes to: Understanding Corporate Finance.** I'd just appreciate your feedback.

Reviews can be tough to come by these days. You, the reader, have the power now to make or break a book. If you have the time, here's a link to my author page on Amazon where you can find all of my books: https://www.amazon.com/-/e/B01JVF2XTU or just search for the title and my name on Amazon. A quick review will be immensely appreciated!

Thank you so much for reading **MBA ASAP 10 Minutes to: Understanding Corporate Finance** and for spending the time and effort with me.

In deep gratitude,

John Cousins

Level Up!

For more business skills and knowledge
check out www.mba-asap.com and sign up
for the our newsletter!

Made in the USA
Las Vegas, NV
30 September 2024

96033379R00042